LOOKING GOOD

THE URBAN ASSEMBLY ACADEMY OF
CIVIC ENGAGEMENT (MS366)
650 HOLLYWOOD AVE
BRONX, NY 10465

Joanne Barkan

Copyright © 2005 Sundance/Newbridge, LLC

All rights reserved. No part of this publication may be reproduced or transmitted in any form or by any means, electronic or mechanical, including photocopy, recording, or any information or retrieval system, without permission in writing from the publisher.

Published by
Sundance Publishing
33 Boston Post Road West
Suite 440
Marlborough, MA 01752
800-343-8204
www.sundancepub.com

Looking Good
ISBN 978-0-7608-9634-1

Illustrations by Brian Biggs

Photo Credits:
Cover (left) Getty Images, (center) Digital Vision/Getty Images, (right) ©Julio Donoso/CORBIS SYGMA; p. 6 (top) ©Mimmo Jodice/CORBIS, (center) ©Bettmann/CORBIS; p. 7 ©Bettmann/CORBIS; p. 8 ©Archivo Iconografico, S.A./CORBIS; p. 9 (top) Kent State University Museum Library Collection, (bottom left, bottom right) Firstview.com; p. 10 (bottom right) ©PoodlesRock/CORBIS; p. 12 (top, bottom) ©CORBIS; p. 13 (top left) ©Reuters/CORBIS, (top right) ©John Springer Collection/CORBIS, (bottom left) ©Bettmann/CORBIS; p. 16 (top left, bottom right) ©Gianni Dagli Orti/CORBIS, (bottom left) ©Archivo Iconografico, S.A./CORBIS; p. 17 (top) ©Roger Wood/CORBIS, (bottom) ©Stefan Klein; p. 18 ©Leonard de Selva/CORBIS; p. 19 (top) The Granger Collection, New York, (bottom) ©Chris Lisle/CORBIS; p. 20 The Granger Collection, New York; p. 21(top) ©John Springer Collection/ CORBIS, (bottom left) ©Mitchell Gerber/CORBIS, (bottom center) ©Lynn Goldsmith/CORBIS, (bottom right) ©Lawrence Manning/CORBIS; p. 24 The Granger Collection, New York; p. 25 (left) Brooklyn Museum, Gift of Mrs. Clarence Hyde, (right) Philip Habib/Getty Images; p. 26 (top, center) courtesy of www.swankvintage.com, (bottom) © Massimo Listri/CORBIS;
p. 27 (left) Paul Fievez/Getty Images, (right) The Metropolitan Museum of Art, New York. Gift of Rose Messing; p. 28 (top) Photodisc/FotoSearch, (bottom) ©Bettmann/CORBIS; p. 29 ©Dennis Degnan/CORBIS; p. 30 (top right, center left, bottom left, bottom right) The Granger Collection, New York

Printed by Nordica International Ltd.
Manufactured in Guangzhou, China
September, 2012
Nordica Job#: CA21201174
Sundance/Newbridge PO#: 227158

Table of Contents

Cool Clothes 4
Really Ancient 6
Extreme Clothing 8
Fashion Freedom 10

Big Wigs and Little Bobs 14
Hairless and Happy 16
The Biggest Big Wigs 18
Carefree at Last 20

Little Extras 22
Stepping Out in Style 24
Hats Off 28

Fact File 30
Glossary 31
Index 32

Cool Clothes

Before you read any further, take a quick look in a mirror.

If you're wearing a pair of pants, do they have wide legs or narrow ones? If you're wearing a shirt, does it have a collar? Why did you choose these fashion styles and not others?

People choose certain clothes because they think the style looks good. And looking good usually means being "in fashion" or "in style." It also means wearing styles that are popular with people around you.

What's "in" is always changing. Some styles are in for a few months; others stay popular for years. Do you like to wear the latest fashions? Some people don't care. But for lots of people, being in style makes them feel better about themselves.

Really Ancient

The earliest humans didn't have clothes like we have today. It wasn't until about 7,000 years ago, when humans learned to weave cloth, that the fashion game really began.

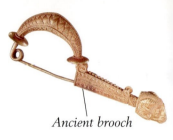

Ancient brooch

Keeping It Simple

In ancient Greece, clothing was kept simple, loose, and graceful. People draped large rectangular pieces of cloth around the body. One large piece of draped cloth became a cloak. A **tunic** was created by attaching two smaller rectangles at the shoulders. Fancy **brooches**, or decorative pins, were used to hold the clothing in place.

For the Greeks, draped clothing was a sign of education and good taste. They considered people who wore pants to be **barbarians**.

Both men and women wore draped clothing. Women's tunics were ankle-length, and men's ended at the knees.

DRAPING A TOGA

①

②

Tale of the Toga

The ancient Romans made the **toga** famous. It was a fine piece of cloth shaped like a half-circle and draped around the body. It began as simple, everyday clothing. But as the Roman Empire grew, so did the toga. It grew into a huge piece of cloth that was 20 feet long—almost as long as a large moving truck!

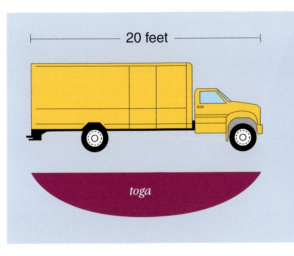

The color of a toga indicated the status, or rank, of the person wearing it.

Extreme Clothing

Humans have always used clothing to show off wealth and power. This can lead to extreme clothing!

Ruff!

Queen Elizabeth I of England loved the extravagant styles of the 1500s. Her clothes were covered with jewels and lace. Her skirts grew bigger and wider as they shot out from her hips. But the most extreme style of all was her **ruff**.

The ruff began as a fancy collar. It grew huge under Elizabeth. Layers of stiff ruffles and lace framed the head like an enormous fan. Behind these layers were two more pieces of decorated cloth. Each piece of cloth was supported by wire. In the middle of the ruff, a person's head looked like a small ball.

Queen Elizabeth's ornate, costly clothing set fashion trends for her times.

Covered in Ribbons

When you think of ribbons used in fashions, you probably think of women's clothing. But in France during the 1600s, men covered themselves with ribbons. Ribbons decorated shirtsleeves and jacket cuffs. The most extreme clothing was a knee-length pair of shorts called petticoat **breeches.** These shorts, almost completely covered with loops of ribbons, were so full they looked like a skirt.

A man's outfit could require hundreds of feet of ribbon.

FASHION REPEATS

Hundreds of years later, this clothing seems to be repeating fashions of the past.

Designer Junya Watanabe created this extreme ruff.

Designer Jean Paul Gaultier created this ribbon evening gown.

Fashion Freedom

Purple pants and silk shirts—you can wear them whenever you want. But if you wore these fashions hundreds of years ago, you'd be breaking the law!

The Price of Purple

Rulers have always tried to show that they are better than other people. Making laws about clothing is one way to do this. In past societies, only the royal family could wear purple. What was so special about purple? The dye came from a rare shellfish, so it was the most expensive color to make.

People have always used clothing to show their place in society. Hundreds of years ago, only nobles could wear furs. And laws were set to determine how many silk clothes a person could own.

It is hard to imagine clothing rules and laws of the past. During modern times, people have been free to choose any fashions they want to wear.

A royal crown with purple fabric

Changing Fashions

Here are some typical and far-out American women's fashions of past decades.

1900s

1920s

1950s

1960s

1970s

How Much Cloth?

For centuries, wealthy men wore long, loose robes. Then in 1340, a sudden change took place. Men started wearing short, tight jackets. These required much less cloth, and cloth merchants started going out of business. Luckily, a new style saved them in the 1360s. It was a long, very full robe called the "houppelande." It used twice as much cloth as the old long robe. The cloth business was soon booming again.

houppelande

Take a Deep Breath

Being in style could be dangerous to your health in the early 1900s. Women wore very tight **corsets** ribbed with whalebone or steel. The corset squeezed the woman's body so it could look "fashionably" shaped. Some women fainted because they couldn't breathe! Doctors warned women that this fashion could injure their spine. But women didn't give up the fashion. The desire to be "in" was stronger than doctors' warnings. The painful corsets vanished when World War I began. Millions of men from America and Europe went into battle. So women took over the men's jobs in offices and factories. They insisted on comfortable, practical clothing. When the war ended, the "new" women refused to go back to the extreme old styles. This trend was repeated during World War II.

A corset

This famous poster of Rosie the Riveter reflected the trend during wartime for practical women's clothing.

STYLE MAKERS

Famous people often make styles popular. In the United States, women have looked to First Ladies for fashion ideas. Jacqueline Kennedy, the wife of President John Kennedy, made the knee-length, A-line dress popular. Famous singers, from Elvis Presley to the latest rap stars, have shaped styles for boys and young men.

TEENS IN JEANS

Before the 1940s, blue jeans were worn as work clothes—they were sturdy and comfortable. But in the mid-1940s, the blue-jean fad began. Thousands of teenagers started showing up on campuses with baggy, rolled-up jeans. Jeans became a fashion. Since then, the style for what kind of jeans are "in" is always changing.

1950s' rolled jeans

Jeans today

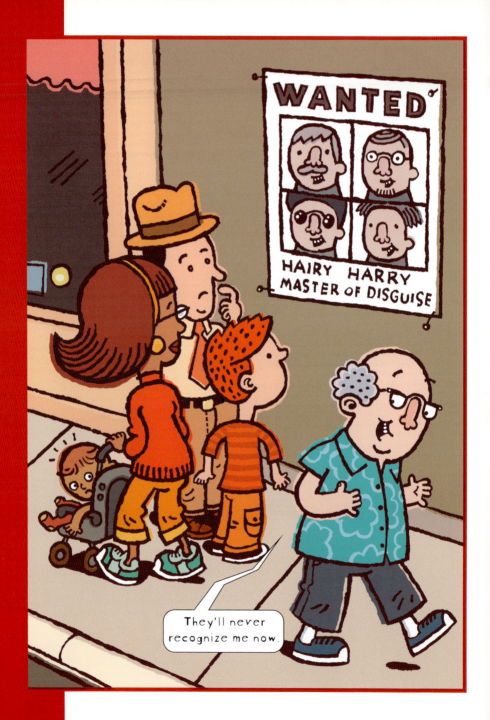

Big Wigs and Little Bobs

Try to describe your best friend. You'll probably say something like this: "She's tall with dark curly hair," or "He has blond hair and blue eyes."

Hair is one of the first things we notice about someone. This makes it an important part of how we look. No wonder humans have always spent so much time on their hair.

If you want to change your look, it's a lot easier to change your hairstyle than it is to change other parts of your body. You can cut your hair if you're too hot or if you feel like you don't fit in. You can even change the shade if you don't like the color! It's no surprise that people have always given hair an important role in the world of style.

Hairless and Happy

Bad hair days didn't exist for some ancient Egyptians. They figured out how to have perfect hair every day. They just didn't use their own hair!

From Head to Toe

Some early Egyptians shaved their body from head to toe! They polished their skin with a fine **pumice**. Then they covered their head with a simple headcloth. But for special events, they got out their big wigs. The wigs were braided and twisted into large shapes. They were a dramatic change from their everyday hairless head.

Many Egyptians shaved their head for comfort and style. But for occasions, they wore wigs made from animal hair or vegetable fibers.

Pharaoh's Beard

The pharaoh was the Egyptian king. Wearing a beard made him stand out in a beardless crowd. So did he grow one? No, he just wore a short, stiff, fake beard that he attached behind his ears!

This golden mask of King Tut shows a beard attachment.

 Why Go Bald?

Some people think Egyptians shaved their head and chose to wear wigs to avoid getting tiny bugs called head lice. Here is an ancient Egyptian recipe to get rid of lice.

Aromatic Head Lice Formula

- 1/2 cup vinegar
- 1/2 cup water
- 12 drops oil of cinnamon
- 12 drops oil of rosemary
- 12 drops oil of terebinth

The Biggest Big Wigs

Imagine a hairstyle so tall that it wouldn't fit through a door! At St. Paul's Cathedral in London, they raised the roof and increased the height of the doorway by four feet. That way, big hairstyles could fit!

Glued Together

By the 1700s, women in most European **courts** wore mountains of hair, but only some of it was their own. The rest was false hair combed over tall wire cages on their head. Going to this extreme for fashion required a lot of work.

Hairdressers used rice powder, flour, and sticky creams to hold wigs all together. The "hairdos" were decorated with ribbons, lace, and flowers. Some even had **miniature** scenes built on the curls and waves, like fleets of small boats in battle.

What an Itch!

With small repairs, a hairdo could last for three weeks. But lice and other bugs could move in long before then. The itching could be terrible. So slits were made in the headdress. Now a servant could slip an ivory wand through the slit and scratch a lady's head!

Poking fun at extreme hairdos

WIGS FOR THE GEISHA

Women who perform traditional entertainment ceremonies in Japan are called geisha. They train for many years to learn the art of Japanese dance, music, storytelling, and tea ceremonies. Geisha wear special clothing, makeup, and wigs.

Carefree at Last

The long struggle with wigs finally came to an end. Men and women returned to something they hadn't used in a long time—their own hair.

Men Go Short

After the French Revolution, fashions took a turn towards a simpler style. Clothes were not as colorful or as extreme. Hairstyles took the same turn. Men got rid of their wigs and shortened their hair. Short hairstyles varied—some were combed forward, and others were parted on the side. Men also began slicking their hair with oil to keep it in place. Men didn't let their hair grow below their ears until about 150 years later—during the hippie days of the 1960s. Then very long hair was "in" again. But there was a big difference in this style—it was all their own hair this time.

The oil used on men's hair stained sofas and chairs, so people draped cloth over their furniture.

Women Are Bobbed

Women threw away their wigs, too. But they still fussed with their hairstyles. This all changed during World War I. Women needed to wear simpler hairstyles when they went to work in the factories. So they cut their hair.

In the 1920s, women broke free of all the fussing and cut their hair very short. The new, boyish hairstyle was called the "bob."

Silent-film star Lulu was one of the first to wear the bob.

HAIR IDENTITY

People often choose hairstyles that express their personality, culture, and the times in which they live.

Dreadlocks

Mohawk

Buzz cut

Little Extras

What do a sun hat and a diamond ring have in common? They're accessories—they dress up an outfit and tell others that you've got style!

Accessories aren't things you need to wear—they are extras. Bags, belts, hair clips, and scarves are all accessories. You can wear an outfit without any of these things. But accessories can add a little fun, beauty, or comfort to your style.

You can go to the beach without a sun hat—but it's useful to have one. You can dress up without a fancy ring, but it might just add a sparkle to your outfit. Even though they're not needed, accessories are "in." So let's go accessorize!

Stepping Out in Style

Walking in some shoes is not just difficult—it's impossible!

Never-Ending Points

Imagine wearing shoes that might be 24 inches longer than your feet. That's what stylish men wore starting in the 1300s. They couldn't walk unless they stiffened the pointed toes with whalebone. The long toes of some metal **sabatons** were controlled by a chain.

Staying Clean and Dry

Walking down a European street in the 1500s was not a pleasant stroll. Without sewers or garbage dumps, the streets were really dirty. People wore long, pointed **pattens** to protect fine shoes and stockings. The patten was just as long and just as pointed as the shoe.

Here is a look at men's shoes worn in the 1400s.

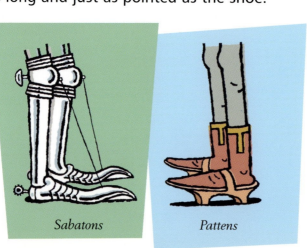

Sabatons

Pattens

Wealthy women in Venice wore big **platform** shoes to protect their feet. Venice was built on canals that sometimes flooded the city. The super-tall shoe—sometimes two-and-a-half feet tall—probably kept a woman's feet dry. But most of all, these shoes were fashion accessories. The stylish woman showed her wealth because she couldn't walk without the help of a servant!

Don't I look fabulous!

Chopines were high-platformed shoes that Venetian women started wearing in the early 1500s.

EXTREME SHOES TODAY
Can you imagine walking in these modern-day shoes?

Extremely New Shoes

People in the past have always created their own extreme shoes, and people in the future will probably do the same. Wealthy famous people have always bought expensive accessories that make them stand out. Marlene Dietrich, a popular movie star of the 1940s, had a special pair of shoes made by a designer in Paris. Each shoe had a ball of diamonds on the heel!

Here is a close-up of a replica of one of Marlene Dietrich's diamond-heeled shoes.

This is an ankle-strap sandal designed in 1938 by Ferragamo.

A hundred years ago, an extreme shoe was only for the very wealthy. But today, modern industry can produce shoes more quickly and for less cost. In the 1970s, buying an extreme pair of glittery platform shoes was affordable for many women.

Modern designers use modern methods to give us shoes that are practical, comfortable, and useful. But they also give us shoes that are impractical, stylized, and funky. So there is something for everyone's fashion style.

The Shoe Hat

Here are two accessories combined into one. This is Elsa Schiaparelli's famous shoe hat, which she designed with artist Salvador Dali.

The design of these hand-painted boots is based on the Beatles film, *Yellow Submarine*.

Hats Off

Getting rid of a fashion while it's still popular is not that easy. But is it any easier to bring back a fashion once it dies out?

Ban the Bird Hat!

Stylish hats were piled high with feathers and stuffed birds in the 1800s. Women wore owls' heads, sparrow wings, and whole hummingbirds. Many people were outraged. The explosive growth of American cities had already destroyed many forests and wildlife in America. Now hatmakers were destroying entire bird populations!

Bird-hat fashion

In 1896, several Boston women began fighting the hat industry. The Audubon Club educated people about protecting birds. They also asked women to stop buying bird hats. Audubon clubs sprang up around the United States. Their work resulted in convincing Congress to pass a law that protected wild animals and birds.

Here, Mary Pickford, one of the first motion picture stars, wears a bird hat.

WHAT'S A FACE EXTRA?

Beauty patches—also called beauty spots—were a big hit in the court of Louis XIV. They were small pieces of black silk with glue on one side. They could be any shape, such as a circle, star, or heart. They were worn on the face by men and women and highlighted the eyes or mouth. They also hid scars and acne. People carried extra patches in fancy little boxes. Each box had a mirror inside the lid.

Bring Them Back?

For many centuries, hats were fashionable accessories for men and women. An outfit wasn't complete if it didn't include a hat. Then suddenly the hat accessory disappeared in the late 1960s. It might be because this was a time of freedom from fashion rules.

The hat industry tried to bring back the hat. It spent huge amounts of money on advertising. Fashion magazines tried to make hats popular again—but nothing worked. Today, "in" fashions no longer demand a hat.

Hats can be worn for protection or just for fun!

Fashions change, but looking good is always in!

Fact File

8th–9th century
Cotton and silk weaving reach Spain from the East.

Germany publishes first fashion magazine. **1586**

Isaac Singer perfects and patents the sewing machine in the United States. **1851**

First machine-made lace is produced. **1760**

1785
First practical power loom is patented.

1900 Special clothes are created for riding in a motor car.

1938
Nylon is first produced by Du Pont; first nylon stockings are made.

Glossary

barbarians people who are considered uncivilized

breeches short pants that attach below the knee

brooches decorative pins

corsets tight undergarments worn to change the shape of the body

courts members of a ruler's family and advisers

miniature very small in size

pattens overshoes worn to protect shoes and stockings

platform a thick layer of cork or wood to raise up something

pumice a light, glasslike material from volcanoes that is used to polish things

ruff a large, lacy collar worn by men and women in the 1500s

sabatons metal armor worn on the feet

toga a large piece of cloth draped around the body

tunic two rectangles of cloth attached at the shoulders

corset

Index

accessories 22–29
Audubon clubs 28
beard 17
beauty patches 29
bird hat 28
breeches 9
brooches 6
clothes 4–11
corsets 12
Egyptians 16–17
fashion time line 30
France 9, 29
geisha 19
Greece 6
hair 14–21
hair bob 21
hats 28–29
jeans 13
lice 17, 19
pharaoh 17
platform shoes 25, 27
purple 10
Queen Elizabeth I 8
ribbons 9
robes 11

Roman Empire 7
ruff 8
shoes 24–27
style makers 13
toga 6–7
tunic 6
Venice 25
wigs 16–19
World War I 12, 21